The All-Day Dumpling Cookbook

Dumpling Recipes for the Home Chef

BY

Carla Hale

License Notes

No part of this Book can be reproduced in any form or by any means including print, electronic, scanning or photocopying unless prior permission is granted by the author.

All ideas, suggestions and guidelines mentioned here are written for informative purposes. While the author has taken every possible step to ensure accuracy, all readers are advised to follow information at their own risk. The author cannot be held responsible for personal and/or commercial damages in case of misinterpreting and misunderstanding any part of this Book

Table of Contents

Introduction

Dumplings are a dish that makes people smile. At their very core, dumplings are not only incredibly easy to make, but they are one of the most wonderfully satisfying foods you can enjoy today. Dumplings are made synonymous with a good time and are perfect to make whenever you are having a gathering with your friends and family.

If you have enjoyed dumplings for yourself, then you will love the contents of this book. Throughout the pages of this cookbook, you will learn not only will you learn how to make dumplings completely from scratch. By the end of this cookbook, I am confident you will become a dumpling making pro in no time.

So, let's stop wasting time and get to cooking!

Old Fashioned Chicken and Dumplings

This is a family favorite meal that is not only comforting, but it is extremely delicious as well. It is easy to make, you will be surprised that it is made completely from scratch.

Makes: 8 servings

Total Prep Time: 1 hour and 45 minutes

Ingredients for the broth:

- 1 rotisserie chicken, whole and cut into small pieces
- 1 onion, thinly sliced
- 3 carrots, cut into pieces
- 3 stalks of celery, thinly sliced
- 8 cups of low sodium chicken broth
- Dash of salt and black pepper
- 1 bay leaf

Ingredients for the dumplings:

- 1 ¾ cups of all-purpose flour
- 1/3 cup of shortening
- ½ tsp. of baker's style baking powder
- ¾ cup of whole milk
- ½ tsp. of salt
- Remaining ingredients:
- 4 Tbsp. of cornstarch
- Parsley, chopped and for garnish

Directions:

1. In a pot, add the shredded rotisserie chicken, chopped carrots and chopped celery. Season with a dash of salt and black pepper. Stir well to mix. Cook over medium heat for 1 minute.

2. Add in the chicken broth.

3. Allow to come to boil. Lower the heat to low. Cook for 45 minutes to 1 hour or until the chicken is soft.

4. Remove the chicken and vegetables from the broth. Set aside.

5. Prepare the dumpling. In a bowl, add in the all-purpose flour, baker's style baking powder, dash of salt and shortening. Stir well to mix. Add in the milk and stir well to mix. Transfer the dough onto a flat surface. Knead for 1 minute or until smooth in consistency.

6. Roll the dough until it is 1/8 inch in thickness. Slice into strips at are 2 inches in size.

7. Add the dumplings into the broth. Cook for 15 to 20 minutes or until the dumplings are soft.

8. Add in the chicken. Cook for 3 minutes or until piping hot.

9. Remove from heat and serve immediately.

Shrimp Dumplings

This is the perfect dumpling recipe for you to make if you love the taste of shrimp. Everybody in the family will love it.

Makes: 30 servings

Total Prep Time: 25 minutes

Ingredients for the dipping sauce:

- ¼ cup of black vinegar
- 2 Tbsp. of low sodium soy sauce
- 1, 1 inch piece of ginger, peeled and thinly sliced
- 1 red chile, seeds removed and chopped

Ingredients for the dumplings:

- ½ pound of shrimp, shell on, peeled and chopped
- ¼ cup of scallion greens, thinly sliced
- 1, 2 inch piece of ginger, peeled and grated
- 2 Tbsp. of low sodium soy sauce
- 1 tsp. of potato starch
- 1 tsp. of white sugar
- 1 tsp. of toasted sesame oil
- ½ tsp. of salt
- Dash of white pepper
- 30 dumpling wrappers

Directions:

1. Prepare the dipping sauce. In a bowl, add in the black vinegar, soy sauce, grated ginger and chopped red chile. Stir well to mix and set aside.

2. Prepare the dumplings. In a food processor, add in the shrimp. Pulse until ¼ inch in size. Transfer into a bowl.

3. In the bowl, add in the sliced scallions, grated ginger, soy sauce, potato starch, white sugar and sesame oil. Season with a dash of salt and black pepper. Stir well to mix.

4. Place the dumpling wrappers onto a flat surface. Fill with 1 teaspoon of the shrimp mix. Fold the wrapper over the filling and pleat the edges to seal. Repeat with the remaining wrappers.

5. In a pot set over medium heat, fill with salted water. Allow to come to a boil. Add in the dumplings. Cook for 4 minutes or until the dumplings begins to float to the surface. Repeat.

6. Drain the dumplings.

7. Serve with the dipping sauce.

Pork and Bok Choy Wonton Soup

This is another delicious Asian style soup dish you can make whenever you are craving something with an authentic Asian flavor.

Makes: 6 servings

Total Prep Time: 30 minutes

Ingredients for the wontons:

- Dash of salt
- 8 ounces of lean ground pork
- 1 Tbsp. of soy sauce
- Dash of white sugar
- 18 wonton wrappers
- 1 ½ pounds of bok choy, rinsed
- 1 tsp. of ginger, minced
- 1 ½ tsp. of Shaoxing wine
- Dash of black pepper

Ingredients for the soup:

- 8 scallions, thinly sliced
- 1/3 cup of ginger, thinly sliced
- 6 dried shiitake mushrooms, soaked for 1 hour
- ¼ cup of Shaoxing wine
- Dash of salt and black pepper
- 3 pounds of chicken necks, backs and wings
- 1 Tbsp. of whole peppercorns
- 12 cups of cold water
- 1 tsp. of soy sauce

Directions:

1. Prepare the wontons. In a pot set over medium to high heat, fill with salted water. Add in the bok choy and cook for 2 minutes or until bright green. Drain and set aside to cool slightly. Squeeze out the excess liquid.

2. Transfer the bok choy into a food processor. Pulse on the highest setting until chopped. Add in the pork and minced ginger. Pulse again until coarse in consistency.

3. Transfer the mix into a bowl. In the bowl, add in the soy sauce, Shaoxing wine and white sugar. Season with a dash of salt and black pepper.

4. Add 1 tablespoon of the filling into the center of the wrapper. Wet the edges of the wrapper with water and fold over the filling. Crimp the edges to seal. Repeat.

5. Prepare the soup. In a stockpot set over medium to high heat, add in the chicken pieces, sliced ginger, whole peppercorns, mushrooms and cold water. Stir well to mix and allow to come to a boil.

6. Lower the heat to low and add in the Shaoxing wine. Cook for 2 ½ hours.

7. Strain the broth into a bowl. Toss out the solids except for the mushrooms. Set the broth aside to cool completely. Place back over medium heat. Add in the soy sauce and reserved mushrooms. Season with a dash of salt and black pepper. Lower the heat to low and cover.

8. In a pot set over medium to high heat, fill with salted water. Allow to come to a boil. Add in the wontons. Cook for 5 minutes or until the wontons begin to float to the surface. Drain and transfer into serving bowls.

9. Pour the broth over the dumplings. Top off with the sliced scallions.

10. Serve.

Classic Pan Fried Dumplings

One bite of these delicious dumplings and you will never want to order boring takeout dumplings ever again.

Makes: 6 servings

Total Prep Time: 1 hour

Ingredients:

- 2 Tbsp. of dried shrimp
- ¼ cup of rice vermicelli
- 3 eggs
- Dash of salt
- 1 Tbsp. of vegetable oil
- 2 bunches of Chinese chives, chopped
- 2 mushrooms, chopped
- 1 Tbsp. of vegetable oil
- ½ tsp. of salt
- ¼ tsp. of sesame oil
- Dash of black pepper
- 40 wonton wrappers
- 1 ¼ cups of water, boiling
- 1 Tbsp. of vegetable oil, as needed

Directions:

1. In a bowl, add in the dried shrimp and cover with the water. Set aside to soak for 30 minutes. Drain and chop into small pieces.

2. In a separate bowl, add the rice vermicelli and cover with warm water. Set aside to rest for 10 minutes. Drain and chop the noodles into small pieces.

3. In a bowl, add in the eggs and season with a dash of salt. Whisk until lightly beaten.

4. In a wok set over medium heat, add in 1 tablespoon of sesame oil. Add in the eggs. Cook for 2 minutes or until the eggs are set. Flip gently and cook for another minute. Remove and set aside to cool completely before chopping into small pieces.

5. In a bowl, add in the egg pieces, shrimp, rice noodles, chopped chives, mushrooms, 1 tablespoon of vegetable oil and sesame oil. Season with a dash of salt and black pepper.

6. Brush the edges of the wonton wrapper with water. Add 1 tablespoon of the egg filling in the center. Fold the wrapper over the filling. Pleat the edges to seal. Repeat.

7. In a skillet set over medium to high heat, add in 1 tablespoon of vegetable oil. Add in the dumplings. Fry for 2 minutes on both sides or until golden.

8. Add in the boiling water and cover. Cook for 10 minutes.

9. Remove and serve immediately.

Pork and Scallion Dumplings

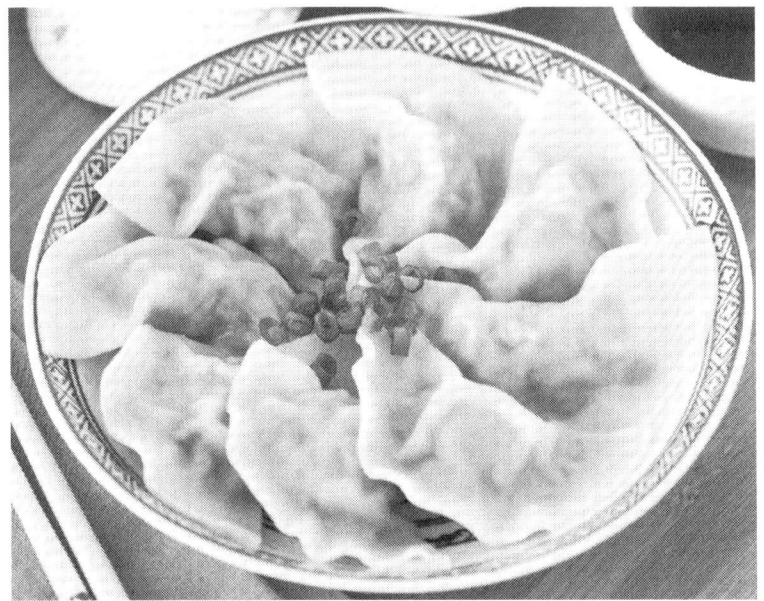

This is a traditional Asian dumpling recipe you can make whenever you are craving takeout. One bite and you will never want to order takeout again.

Makes: 75 servings

Total Prep Time: 20 minutes

Ingredients:

- 1 pound of pork should, cut into cubes
- 1 ½ tsp. of salt
- ¼ pound of bacon, cut into pieces
- 1 egg
- 2 Tbsp. of chicken stock
- 1 Tbsp. of Shaoxing wine
- 2 tsp. of soy sauce
- ½ tsp. of white sugar
- 16 scallions, thinly sliced
- 75 dumpling wrappers, store-bought

Directions:

1. In a bowl, add the pork cubes and dash of salt. Toss well to mix. Spread onto a baking sheet. Place into the freezer to freeze for 15 minutes.

2. In the bowl of a food processor, add in the pork, bacon, chicken stock, egg, soy sauce and white sugar. Pulse on the highest setting until pureed. Add in the leeks and pulse again until incorporated.

3. Place the dumpling wrappers onto a flat surface. Add 1 tablespoon of the filling into the center of the water. Fold the wrapper over the filling. Pleat the edges to seal. Repeat with the remaining filling and dumpling wrappers.

4. In a pot set over medium heat, fill with salted water. Allow to come to a boil. Place a bamboo steamer over the water and add the dumplings into the steam. Steam for 8 to 10 minutes or until cooked through.

5. Remove and serve immediately.

Spicy Pork Dumplings

Make these delicious dumplings whenever you are craving something that is packed full of flavor.

Makes: 4 servings

Total Prep Time: 30 minutes

Ingredients:

- ¼ pound of lean ground pork
- 2 ounces of shrimp, shells removed and chopped
- 1 egg white
- ¼ cup of water chestnut, minced
- 2 Tbsp. of celery, minced
- 1 tsp. of cilantro, minced
- ½ tsp. of ginger, minced
- ½ tsp. of white sugar
- ½ tsp. of salt
- 1/8 tsp. of sesame oil
- Dash of white pepper
- 24 dumpling wrappers
- 3 Tbsp. of vegetable oil
- ½ to 2/3 cup of chicken broth

Ingredients for the sauce:

- 1 ½ Tbsp. of soy sauce
- 1 Tbsp. of seasoned rice vinegar
- 1 Tbsp. of chili and garlic sauce
- 1 tsp. of hot chili oil

Directions:

1. Prepare the filling. In a bowl, add in the lean pork, shrimp, egg white, chestnuts, minced celery, minced cilantro, ginger, white sugar, dash of salt and sesame oil. Season with a dash of black pepper. Stir well to mix.

2. Place the dumpling wrappers onto a flat surface.

3. Add a tablespoon of the filling into the center of the wrappers. Brush the edges of the wrapper with water. Fold over the filling and crimp the edges with a fork to seal. Repeat and place the dumplings onto a baking sheet.

4. In a skillet set over medium to high heat, add in 1 ½ tablespoons of vegetable oil. Add in the dumplings and cook for 5 minutes or until crispy.

5. Add in 1/3 cup of the broth. Lower the heat to low and cook for 5 minutes or until the broth has been absorbed. Transfer onto a plate.

6. Prepare the sauce. In a bowl, add in the soy sauce, seasoned rice vinegar, chili and garlic sauce and chili oil. Whisk well until smooth in consistency.

7. Serve the dumplings with the sauce.

Chard Dumplings

These dumplings are packed with a healthy mix of Swiss chard, mushrooms and scallions, to make a dumpling dish you don't have to feel guilty about enjoying.

Makes: 24 servings

Total Prep Time: 1 hour

Ingredients:

- 1 Tbsp. + 1 tsp. of vegetable oil
- 4 ounces of shiitake mushrooms, chopped
- 2 cloves of garlic, minced
- 1 tsp. of sesame oil, toasted
- Dash of salt and black pepper
- 8 ounces of Swiss chard
- 2 scallions, thinly sliced
- 2 tsp. of rice wine vinegar
- 1 tsp. of low sodium soy sauce
- 24 dumpling wrappers

Directions:

1. In a skillet set over medium to high heat, add in 1 teaspoon of vegetable. Add in the Swiss chard, chopped mushrooms, chopped scallions and minced garlic. Stir well to mix. Cook for 5 minutes or until the liquid has evaporated.

2. Squeeze out the excess liquid. Transfer into a bowl.

3. In the bowl, add in the rice wine vinegar, toasted sesame oil and soy sauce. Stir well to mix. Season with a dash of salt and black pepper.

4. Wipe the skillet clean with a few paper towels.

5. Place a dumpling wrapper onto a flat surface. Place 1 teaspoon of the filling into the center. Moisten the edges with water. Fold over the filling. Crimp the edges with a fork to seal. Repeat and transfer the dumplings onto a baking sheet.

6. In the skillet, add in 1 tablespoon of vegetable oil. Set back over medium to high heat. Add in the dumplings. Cook for 3 minutes on each side or until golden.

7. Add in ½ cup of water. Cover and cook for 6 minutes or until the water evaporates completely.

8. Remove from heat and serve.

Pork and Cabbage Dumplings

These homemade dumplings are easier and faster to make than most homemade dumplings that you can make.

Makes: 40 servings

Total Prep Time: 1 hour

Ingredients for the dumplings:

- 1 pound of napa cabbage, minced
- 1 Tbsp. of salt, evenly divided
- 1 pound of lean pork shoulder
- 1 tsp. of white pepper
- 1 Tbsp. of garlic, minced
- 1 tsp. of ginger, minced
- 2 ounces of scallions, minced
- 2 tsp. of white sugar
- 40 dumpling wrappers
- Vegetable oil, for cooking

Ingredients for the sauce:

- ½ cup of rice vinegar
- ¼ cup of soy sauce
- 2 Tbsp. of chili oil

Directions:

1. Prepare the dumplings. In a bowl, add in the minced cabbage and 2 teaspoons of salt. Toss well to mix. Transfer into a strainer and set aside to drain for 15 minutes. Wring out the excess moisture from the cabbage.

2. In a separate bowl, add in the pork, drained cabbage, 1 teaspoon of salt, dash of white pepper, minced garlic, minced ginger, minced scallions and white sugar. Knead well until evenly mixed.

3. Place the wrappers onto a flat surface. Add 1 tablespoon of the filling and fold the wrapper over the filling. Pleat the edges to seal. Repeat with the remaining wrappers.

4. In a skillet set over medium to high heat, add 1 tablespoon of the vegetable oil. Add in the dumplings and cook for 1 to 2 minutes or until golden brown.

5. Add in ½ cup of water to the skillet. Cover and cook for 5 minutes to steam.

6. Transfer the cooked dumplings onto a plate.

7. Prepare the sauce. In a bowl, add in the rice vinegar, soy sauce and chili oil. Stir well to mix.

8. Serve the dumplings with the sauce.

Pan Fried Leek Dumplings

This is a highly popular Taiwanese dumpling dish that I know you are going to love. They are pan fried and steamed, giving them a crunch that is irresistible.

Makes: 4 servings

Total Prep Time: 30 minutes

Ingredients for the crust:

- 1 cup of all-purpose flour, extra for dusting
- ¼ tsp. of salt
- 1 Tbsp. of vegetable oil
- 1/3 cup of water

Ingredients for the filling:

- 1 Tbsp. of shrimp
- 4 to 6 leeks, chopped
- 2 Tbsp. of vegetable oil
- ½ tsp. of salt, extra for seasoning
- ¼ pound of dried mung bean noodles
- 1 tsp. of sesame oil
- ¼ tsp. of white pepper, extra for seasoning

Ingredients for cooking:

- 2 Tbsp. of vegetable oil
- ½ cup of water

Directions:

1. Prepare the crust. In a bowl, add in the all-purpose flour and dash of salt. Add in the vegetable oil and stir well until a dough begins to form. Place the dough onto a flat surface. Knead the dough for 8 minutes or until smooth in consistency.

2. Cover the dough and set aside to rest for 30 minutes.

3. Prepare the filling. In a bowl, add in the shrimp and ¼ cup of water. Set aside to rest for 5 minutes or until soft. Drain the shrimp and chop into small pieces.

4. In a skillet set over medium to high heat, add in the vegetable oil. Add in the shrimp and cook for 30 seconds. Add in the chopped leeks. Season with a dash of salt. Cook for 10 minutes or until soft.

5. Prepare the noodles according to the directions on the package. Once cooked, drain the noodles and chop.

6. In a separate bowl, add in the cooked leek mix and cooked noodles. Add in the sesame oil and a dash of white pepper. Stir well to mix.

7. Shape the dough into 8 pieces. Roll the pieces until 4 inches in size.

8. Fill each dough piece with 1 tablespoon of filling. Fold the dough around the filling. Crimp the edges to seal. Repeat.

9. In a skillet set over medium to high heat, add in 2 tablespoons of vegetable oil. Add in the dumplings. Cook for 5 minutes or until golden.

10. Add the water into the skillet and cover. Steam the dumplings for 8 minutes.

11. Remove and serve immediately.

Potato Dumplings with Brown Butter

This is a traditional dumpling dish that you can make that is made with nutty flavored brown butter. It is a dish that every pierogi lover will love.

Makes: 12 servings

Total Prep Time: 25 minutes

Ingredients for the dumpling dough:

- 1 egg, beaten
- 1 cup of whole milk
- 5 cups of all-purpose flour
- 2 Tbsp. of sour cream
- 1 cup of water
- Yellow cornmeal, for dusting

Ingredients for the filling:

- 5 pounds Yukon gold potatoes, peeled and cut into quarters
- 8 ounces of cream cheese
- Dash of salt and black pepper
- 4 Tbsp. of butter, melted

Ingredients for the brown butter:

- 2 sticks of butter

Directions:

1. Prepare the dumpling dough. In a bowl, add in the egg and sour cream. Add in the whole milk and water. Whisk well to mix. Add in the flour and stir well until a dough begins to form.

2. Place the dough onto a flat surface. Knead for 1 minute.

3. Transfer the dough into a bowl. Cover and set aside to rest for 1 hour.

4. Divide the dough into 4 pieces.

5. Dust a baking sheet with cornmeal.

6. Place the dough onto a flat surface. Roll until 1/8 inch in thickness. Cut out circles that are 3 inches in size from the dough.

7. Prepare the filling. In a pot set over medium to high heat, fill with salted water. Allow to come to a boil. Cook for 8 to 10 minutes or until soft. Drain the potatoes and transfer into a bowl. Mash well until smooth in consistency.

8. In the bowl, add in the cream cheese and butter. Season with a dash of salt and black pepper. Stir well to incorporate.

9. Spread 1 tablespoon of the filling into the dumpling dough. Fold the dough over and crimp with a fork to seal. Repeat.

10. In a skillet set over medium to high heat, add 1 tablespoon of the vegetable oil. Add in the dumplings and cook for 1 to 2 minutes or until golden brown.

11. Add in ½ cup of water to the skillet. Cover and cook for 5 minutes to steam.

12. Transfer the cooked dumplings onto a plate.

13. Prepare the brown butter. In a saucepan set over medium heat, add in the butter. Cook for 8 to 10 minutes or until the butter turns brown.

14. Drizzle the brown butter over the dumplings and serve.

Vanilla and Raisin Dumplings

These are the perfect dumplings for you to make whenever you have a strong sweet tooth that needs to be satisfied.

Makes: 8 servings

Total Prep Time: 40 minutes

Ingredients:

- 8 cups of all-purpose flour
- 1 cup of white sugar
- 2 Tbsp. of baker's style baking powder
- 1 tsp. of salt
- 1, 15 ounce pack of raisins
- 1 1/2, 12 ounce cans of evaporated milk
- 2 cups of molasses
- 1 tsp. of pure vanilla
- ¾ cup of lard, melted

Directions:

1. In a bowl, add in the all-purpose flour, white sugar, baker's style baking powder, dash of salt and raisins. Stir well to mix. Add in the lard and stir well until crumbled.

2. In a separate bowl, add in the evaporated milk, molasses and pure vanilla. Stir well to mix. Add into the flour mix and stir well until the dough begins to form.

3. In a pot set over medium to high heat, fill with water and allow to come to a boil.

4. Divide the dough into small pieces. Add into the water and cover.

5. Lower the heat to low and cook for 35 minutes. Drain and pat dry with a few paper towels.

6. Serve.

Steamed Pork and Shrimp Dumplings

This is a dumpling dish that incorporate 2 of the most classic dumpling flavors you can use. It is packed with an authentic Chinese flavor I know you will love.

Makes: 6 servings

Total Prep Time: 2 hours

Ingredients:

- ¼ pound of shrimp, shells removed
- 1 Tbsp. of baker's style baking soda
- ½ pound of pork, boneless and cut into cubes
- 2 ounces of pork fat
- ¼ tsp. of white pepper
- ½ tsp. of salt
- 2 tsp. of cornstarch
- 2 tsp. of Shaoxing wine
- 1 tsp. of toasted sesame oil
- 1 tsp. of extra virgin olive oil
- ½ tsp. of ginger, peeled and grated
- ½ tsp. of white sugar
- 1 pack of wonton wrappers
- 1 carrot, thinly sliced

Directions:

1. In a bowl, add in the shrimp. Cover with cold water. Add in the baking soda and stir well to incorporate.

2. Cover and set into the fridge to chill for 30 minutes. Drain the shrimp and pat dry with a few paper towels.

3. Transfer the shrimp into a food processor. Pulse until chopped. Transfer into a bowl.

4. In the food processor, add in the pork and pork fat. Pulse until chopped. Transfer into the bowl.

5. In the bowl, add in the white pepper, dash of salt, cornstarch, Shaoxing wine, sesame oil, extra virgin olive oil and grated ginger. Stir well to mix. Cover and place into the fridge to chill for 30 minutes.

6. Place the wonton wrappers onto a flat surface. Add 1 tablespoon of the filling into the center of the wrappers. Fold the wrapper over the filling and crimp the edges to seal. Repeat with the remaining wrappers.

7. In a pot set over medium to high heat, fill with salted water. Allow to come to a boil. Place a steamer basket over the water and add in the dumplings. Cover and allow to steam for 8 minutes or until cooked through.

8. Remove the dumplings and serve.

Stuffed Prune Dumplings

These dumplings are perfect for those who suffer from sensitive stomachs. The prunes in these dumplings can help alleviate upset stomachs and support optimal GI tract.

Makes: 6 servings

Total Prep Time: 20 minutes

Ingredients:

- 4 russet potatoes
- ½ tsp. of salt
- 1 Tbsp. of butter, soft
- 2 eggs, beaten
- ¼ cup of farina
- 1 cup of all-purpose flour
- 12 Italian prunes
- 12 cubes of white sugar
- ½ cup of butter, melted
- ¼ cup of white sugar
- 1 cup of dried breadcrumbs
- Butter, melted and for garnish
- White sugar and for garnish

Directions:

1. In a pot set over medium to high heat, fill with salted water. Allow to come to a boil. Add in the potatoes. Cook for 20 to 25 minutes or until the potatoes are soft. Drain the potatoes and set into a bowl. Mash until smooth in consistency.

2. In the bowl with the potatoes, add the dash of salt, beaten egg, butter, farina and all-purpose flour. Stir well to mix.

3. Transfer the dough onto a flat surface. Knead the dough for 1 minute or until smooth in consistency.

4. Slice the plums and toss out the insides. Place the sugar cubes on the inside of the plums.

5. Roll the dough until it reaches ¼ inch in thickness. Slice into squares that are inches in size.

6. In the center of each square, add in the plums. Roll the dough over the plums and crimp the edges with a fork to seal. Repeat.

7. In a skill set over medium heat, add ½ cup of butter. Allow to melt. Add in the breadcrumbs and ¼ cup of white sugar. Cook for 5 minutes or until golden. Drain the breadcrumbs and set aside.

8. In the bowl with the breadcrumbs, add in the dumplings. Toss gently to coat.

9. Serve.

Homemade Wonton Soup

This is a dish that is typically found in most Asian markets. This is a dish that can be prepared ahead of time if you need to save yourself on time.

Makes: 4 servings

Total Prep Time: 3 ½ hours

Ingredients for the broth:

- 2 pounds of chicken backs and wings, chopped
- 1 ½ pound of pig trotters, thinly sliced
- 3 ounces of Chinese ham
- 1, 3 to 4 inch piece of kombu
- 1 ounce of dried shrimp
- 8 scallions, whites and green parts separated
- 1, 4 inch piece of ginger, thinly sliced
- 12 leaves of napa cabbage, cut into pieces and evenly divided
- Dash of salt

Ingredients for wontons:

- 24 shrimp, shells removed
- ½ tsp. of baker's style baking soda
- ¾ pound of lean ground pork
- 2 tsp. of white sugar
- 1 tsp. of soy sauce
- 2 tsp. of sesame oil
- ½ cup of yellow chives, thinly sliced and evenly divided
- 24 wonton wrappers

Directions:

1. Prepare the broth. In a stockpot set over high heat, add in the chicken, pork trotters and ham. Cover with water and allow to come to a boil. Cook for 10 minutes. Drain the liquid and rinse under water.

2. Cover again with water by at least 1 inch.

3. Add in the kombu, dried shrimp, white parts of the scallion, 1, 4 inch piece of ginger and 4 cabbage leaves. Stir well to mix. Allow to come to a boil. Lower the heat to low and cook for 2 hours.

4. Toss out the bones from the broth. Strain the mix into a saucepan.

5. Prepare the wontons. In a bowl, add in the shrimp, baker's style baking soda, dash of salt and ¼ cup of water. Stir well to mix. Set aside to rest for 15 minutes. Drain.

6. In a bowl, add in the pork, 2 teaspoons of grated ginger, white sugar, soy sauce, sesame oil, half of the chives and dash of salt. Stir well to mix.

7. On a flat surface, add the wonton wrappers. Add 1 tablespoon of the pork mix. Fold the wrapper over the filling. Crimp the edges to seal. Repeat with the remaining wonton wrappers.

8. Allow the broth to come back to a boil. Add in the wontons and cabbage. Cook for 5 minutes or until the wontons are cooked through.

9. Add in the chives and stir well to incorporate. Remove from heat and allow to cool for 1 minute.

10. Serve.

Traditional Matzo Ball Soup

This is a great tasting dumpling dish that you can make to show off your cooking skills to your friends and family.

Makes: 4 servings

Total Prep Time: 35 minutes

Ingredients:

- 32 ounces of chicken broth
- Dash of salt and black pepper
- 1 cup of matzo meal
- 4 eggs, separated
- ¼ cup of seltzer water
- 4 carrots, thinly sliced
- Sprigs of dill, for serving

Directions:

1. Prepare the matzo balls. In a bowl, add in ¼ cup of the chicken broth, egg yolks, dash of salt and black pepper. Whisk well to mix.

2. Add in the seltzer water and matzo meal. Fold gently to incorporate.

3. In a separate bowl, add in the egg whites. Beat with an electric mixer until peaks begin to form on the surface. Add into the egg yolk mix. Fold gently to incorporate.

4. Cover and place into the fridge to chill for 20 minutes.

5. In a pot set over medium heat, fill with salted water. Allow to come to a boil.

6. Roll the matzo mix into 1 inch sized balls. Place into the boiling water. Lower the heat to low and cover. Cook for 25 to 30 minutes or until soft.

7. In a separate pot, add in the remaining chicken broth. Season with a dash of salt. Add in the carrots and cook for 8 minutes or until soft.

8. Drain the matzo balls and place into serving bowls. Pour the broth with the carrots over the top. Serve immediately.

Dumpling Casserole

This is the perfect dish for you to make whenever you have a large group of people that you need to feed. One bite and everybody who tries it will be begging you for the recipe.

Makes: 8 servings

Total Prep Time: 1 hour and 10 minutes

Ingredients:

- 2 cups of mashed potatoes
- 1 cup of all-purpose flour
- 2 eggs, beaten
- 1 ½ tsp. of salt
- Dash of black pepper
- 1 onion, chopped
- 3 Tbsp. of butter, soft
- 2 Tbsp. of all-purpose flour
- 1 cup of heavy whipping cream
- 1 cup of chicken broth
- ½ cup of grated Parmesan cheese
- ½ cup of Jarlsberg cheese, shredded

Directions:

1. In a bowl, add in the mashed potatoes, 1 cup of all-purpose flour and eggs. Season with a dash of salt and black pepper. Stir well to mix.

2. In a pot filled with salted water, set over high heat. Allow to come to a boil. Spoon the dough by the spoonful into the boiling water. Cook for 5 minutes or until the dumplings begin to float to the surface.

3. Drain the dumplings and transfer into a baking dish.

4. Preheat the oven to 350 degrees.

5. In a skillet set over medium heat, add in the butter. Once it melts, add in the onion. Cook for 5 minutes or until soft. Add in the all-purpose flour and cook for an additional minute.

6. Add in the heavy whipping cream and chicken broth. Stir well to mix. Cook for 5 minutes or until thick in consistency.

7. Add the grated parmesan cheese and half of the shredded Jarlsberg cheese over the top. Stir well to mix. Sprinkle the remaining Jarlsberg cheese over the top.

8. Place into the oven to bake for 50 minutes.

9. Remove and serve immediately.

Turkish Yogurt Dumplings

This is a dumpling recipe you can make whenever you want something different in flavor to try. Make to show off your cooking skills to your friends and family.

Makes: 6 servings

Total Prep Time: 1 hour and 5 minutes

Ingredients:

- 2 cups of all-purpose flour
- ½ tsp. of salt
- 2 eggs
- ½ tsp. of water, as needed
- 2 onions, peeled
- ½ pound of lean ground beef
- Dash of salt and black pepper
- 3 Tbsp. of vegetable oil
- 1 Tbsp. of red pepper flakes
- 1 Tbsp. of garlic, minced
- 1, 8 ounce container of plain yogurt

Directions:

1.In a bowl, add in the salt and flour. Stir well to mix. Add in the eggs and water. Stir well until a smooth dough begins to form.

2. Cover the dough and set aside to rest for 35 minutes.

3. In a separate bowl, add in the onion, lean beef, dash of salt and black pepper. Stir well to mix.

4. Divide the dough in half. Place onto a flat surface and roll into a large rectangle and ¼ inch in thickness. Slice into 2 inch squares.

5. In each square, add in 2 teaspoons of the filling into the center of each square. Fold over the filling. Crimp the edges to seal. Repeat with the remaining dough square.

6. In a saucepan set over medium heat, add in the vegetable oil. Add in the crushed red peppers and cook for 2 minutes. Remove from heat and set aside.

7. In a bowl, add in the garlic and plain yogurt. Stir well to mix. Set aside.

8. In a pot set over medium heat, add fill with salted water. Allow to come to a boil. Add in the dumpling. Cook for 20 to 25 minutes. Remove and transfer onto a plate.

9. Drizzle the chili oil over the top of the dumplings.

10. Serve with the yogurt sauce.

Creamy Chicken Stew with Dumplings

Make this delicious stew whenever you are feeling under the weather. The dumplings help to make this stew even more filling.

Makes: 4 servings

Total Prep Time: 45 minutes

Ingredients:

- 1 ½ cups of whole milk
- 1 cup of green peas and carrots
- 1 cup of chicken, cooked and chopped
- 1, 10.75 ounce can of condensed cream of chicken and mushroom soup
- 1 cup of Bisquick mix
- 1/3 cup of whole milk
- Smoked paprika, for seasoning

Directions:

1. In a saucepan set over medium heat, add in the whole milk, green peas and carrots, cooked chicken and can of soup. Stir well to mix. Allow to come to a boil.

2. In a bowl, add in the Bisquick mix and 1/3 cup of whole milk. Stir well until the dough begins to form.

3. Divide the dough into 8 pieces.

4. Drop the dough into the stew. Cook for 10 to 15 minutes or until cooked through.

5. Cover and continue to cook for an extra 10 to 12 minutes.

6. Remove from heat and serve immediately.

Tomato Soup with Buttermilk Dumplings

This is another dish that you can make whenever you want something on the filling side. Serve with bread for the tastiest results.

Makes: 6 servings

Total Prep Time: 50 minutes

Ingredients for the soup:

- 1 Tbsp. of extra virgin olive oil
- ½ of a yellow onion, chopped
- 2 cloves of garlic, minced
- 1 tsp. of dried Italian seasoning
- 1, 28 ounce can of tomatoes, crushed
- 2 cups of water, evenly divided
- 2 tsp. of salt

Ingredients for the dumplings:

- ¾ cup of all-purpose flour
- 1 tsp. of baker's style baking powder
- ¼ tsp. of salt
- ¼ tsp. of black pepper, extra for seasoning
- ¼ cup of sharp cheddar cheese, shredded
- ½ cup of buttermilk
- 2 Tbsp. of Italian parsley, chopped

Directions:

1. Preheat the oven to 350 degrees.

2. In a pot set over medium heat, add in the extra virgin olive oil. Add in the onion and cook for 5 minutes or until soft.

3. Add in the minced garlic and dried Italian seasoning. Cook for an additional minute.

4. Add in the can of crushed tomatoes and 1 cup of water. Allow to come to a simmer.

5. Lower the heat to low and cook for 15 minutes.

6. Transfer into a food processor. Blend on the highest setting until smooth in consistency. Pour back into the pot. Allow to come to a simmer.

7. In a bowl, add in the all-purpose flour, baker's style baking powder, dash of salt, shredded cheddar cheese, dash of salt and black pepper. Add in the buttermilk and stir well until a dough begins to form.

8. Drop the dumpling dough by the spoonful into the pot.

9. Transfer into the oven to cook for 25 minutes.

10. Remove and serve immediately.

Feta Stuffed Dumplings

Make these savory dumplings whenever you make your next Italian feast. Stuffed full of feta cheese, this is a dish that everybody will love.

Makes: 6 servings

Total Prep Time: 40 minutes

Ingredients:

- 3 ½ cups of all-purpose flour
- 2 tsp. of baker's style baking powder
- ½ cup of canola oil
- ¼ cup of butter, melted
- 1 cup of plain yogurt
- 3 eggs
- 1 Tbsp. of sour cream
- 1 Tbsp. of white sugar
- 1 ½ tsp. of salt
- 1 cup of feta cheese, crumbled
- 1 cup of parsley, chopped
- 1 Tbsp. of extra virgin olive
- 2 tsp. of smoked paprika
- 2 egg yolks
- 2 Tbsp. of sesame seeds

Directions:

1. Preheat the oven to 375 degrees. Place a sheet of parchment paper onto a baking sheet.

2. In a bowl, add in the all-purpose flour and baker's style baking soda. Stir well to mix.

3. In a separate bowl, add in the canola oil, butter, yogurt, eggs, white sugar, sour cream and dash of salt. Stir well to mix. Add in the flour mix and stir well until a dough begin to form.

4. Place the dough on a flat surface and knead for 1 minutes or until soft.

5. In a separate bowl, add in the feta cheese, chopped parsley, extra virgin olive oil and smoked paprika. Stir well to mix.

6. Shape the dough into balls that are 2 ½ tablespoons thick. Flatten until 3 inches wide.

7. Add 1 tablespoon of the filling in the center pf the dumpling dough. Fold the dough over the filling. Pinch the edges to seal. Transfer onto a baking sheet.

8. In a bowl, add in the egg yolks. Whisk well until lightly beaten. Brush over the dumplings. Top off with sesame seeds.

9. Place into the oven to bake for 30 minutes.

10. Remove and serve immediately.

Paprika Chicken and Parsley Dumplings

This is the perfect dish for you to make whenever you want to spoil your significant other with something special.

Makes: 4 servings

Total Prep Time: 1 hour and 30 minutes

Ingredients:

- 3 Tbsp. of vegetable shortening
- 1 cup of all-purpose flour
- 2 tsp. of salt
- 1 tsp. of smoked paprika
- 1/8 tsp. of black pepper
- 2 ½ pounds of chicken pieces, bone-in
- 2, 10.5 ounce cans of cream of chicken soup
- 3 cups of whole milk

Ingredients for the dumplings:

- 2 cups of Bisquick
- 2/3 cup of whole milk
- ½ tsp. of dried parsley
- ¼ tsp. of poultry seasoning

Directions:

1. In a saucepan set over medium heat, add in the shortening. Allow to melt.

2. In a bowl, add in 1 cup of all-purpose flour, dash of salt, smoked paprika and dash of black pepper. Stir well to mix. Season the chicken pieces with the mix. Transfer into the shortening. Cook for 8 minutes or until golden.

3. In a separate saucepan set over medium heat, add in the whole milk and cans of soup. Stir well to mix. Allow to come to a boil.

4. Lower the heat. Add in the cooked chicken. Cover and cook for 50 minutes.

5. In a separate bowl, add in the Bisquick, whole milk, dried parsley and poultry seasoning. Stir well until a dough begins to form.

6. Drop the dough by 2 inch sized pieces into the soup. Cook for 15 minutes. Cover and continue to cook for an additional 15 minutes.

7. Remove and serve immediately.

Garam Masala Dumplings

hese delicious dumplings contain a spicy flavor that is impossible to resist. Make them whenever you need something with a bit of a kick.

Makes: 6 servings

Total Prep Time: 20 minutes

Ingredients:

- 1 pound of lean ground pork
- 1 onion, chopped
- ½ a bunch of cilantro, chopped
- ½ tsp. of crushed red pepper flakes
- 2 tsp. of red curry paste
- ½ tsp. of garam masala
- ½ tsp. of powdered chili
- ¼ tsp. of powdered onion
- ¼ tsp. of powdered garlic
- 1 cup of all-purpose flour
- ¼ cup of water, as needed
- 3 Tbsp. of creamy peanut butter
- ½ tsp. of cayenne pepper
- 1 tsp. of white sugar
- 1 tsp. of vegetable oil

Directions:

1. In a bowl, add in the ground pork, chopped onion, chopped cilantro, crushed red pepper flakes, red curry pasta, garam masala, powdered chili, powdered onion and powdered garlic. Stir well to mix.

2. In a separate bowl, add in the all-purpose flour and dash of salt. Add in the water and stir well until a smooth dough forms.

3. Transfer the dough onto a flat surface. Chop the dough into pieces the size of walnuts. Roll the pieces into 3 inch pieces.

4. Add 1 tablespoon of the filling in the center of each dough circles. Top off with another dough circle and pinch the edges to seal. Repeat.

5. In a pot set over medium to high heat, add in 1 inch of water. Place a steamer over the water. Add the dumplings into the steamer. Steam for 10 to 15 minutes.

6. In a bowl, add in the creamy peanut butter, cayenne pepper, white sugar and vegetable oil. Whisk well until smooth in consistency.

7. Serve the dumplings immediately with the sauce.

Tofu Dumplings

Make these delicious dumplings for those vegan and vegetarian members in your household. They are so delicious, even meat eaters will love these dumplings.

Makes: 8 servings

Total Prep Time: 25 minutes

Ingredients:

- 1 ounce of dried shiitake mushrooms, chopped
- 1 pack of firm tofu, drained
- 1 Tbsp. of vegetable oil
- 1 Tbsp. of sesame oil
- 1 Tbsp. of ginger, minced
- 3 cloves of garlic, minced
- 4 scallions, minced
- ¼ tsp. of crushed red chili flakes
- ¼ tsp. of salt
- ¼ tsp. of black pepper
- 2 Tbsp. of soy sauce
- 2 Tbsp. of cilantro, minced
- 30 wonton wrappers
- 1 Tbsp. of cornstarch
- 4 Tbsp. of water

Ingredients for the sauce:

- 2 Tbsp. of sesame oil
- 1 ½ tsp. of chili oil
- 3 cloves of garlic, minced
- ½ tsp. of crushed red chili flakes
- 2 Tbsp. of rice vinegar
- ½ cup of soy sauce
- 1 cup of water
- ¼ cup of honey
- 1 tsp. of cornstarch
- 2 limes, juice only
- 2 Tbsp. of cilantro, minced

Directions:

1. In a bowl, add in the mushrooms and cover with boiling water. Set aside to soak for 1 hour. Drain and chop the mushrooms into small pieces. Set aside.

2. Drain the tofu and crumble into small pieces.

3. In a skillet set over medium to high heat, add in the vegetable oil and sesame oil. Add in the minced garlic, minced ginger, crushed red pepper flakes and chopped scallions. Cook for 5 minutes or until golden.

4. Add in the tofu pieces, dash of black pepper and soy sauce. Cook for 8 minutes or until the tofu is golden. Remove from heat and add in the chopped cilantro. Stir well to mix.

5. In a bowl, add in the cornstarch and water. Whisk until smooth in consistency.

6. Place a wonton wrapper onto a flat surface. Add 1 teaspoon of the filling into the center. Brush the cornstarch mix along the edge of the wrappers. Fold over the filling. Crimp the edges to seal.

7. In a skillet set over medium to high heat, add in the sesame oil. Add in the wontons and fry for 5 minutes or until golden on both sides. Remove and drain on a plate lined with paper towels.

8. Prepare the sauce. In a pot set over low to medium heat, add in all of the ingredients for the sauce. Whisk well until smooth in consistency and allow to come to a simmer. Remove and set aside to cool completely.

9. Serve the dumplings with the sauce.

Turkey Dumplings

This is a wonderful dumpling recipe for you to make right around the Thanksgiving season. It is filling and incredibly easy to make.

Makes: 80 servings

Total Prep Time: 20 minutes

Ingredients:

- 1 pound of lean ground turkey
- ¼ cup of soy sauce
- ¼ cup of white vinegar
- 5 scallions, chopped
- 1, 10 ounce pack of button mushrooms, chopped
- All-purpose flour, for dusting
- 2 Tbsp. of canola oil
- ½ of a head of iceberg lettuce, chopped
- 1 Tbsp. of sesame oil
- 1 Tbsp. of white sugar
- 2 eggs
- Dash of salt and black pepper
- 2, 12 ounce pack of dumpling wrappers

Directions:

1. In a bowl, add in the lean ground turkey, chopped lettuce, soy sauce, sesame oil, white vinegar, white sugar, chopped scallions, eggs and chopped button mushrooms. Season with a dash of salt. Stir well to mix.

2. Dust a baking sheet with flour.

3. Place the dumpling wrappers onto a flat surface. Add 1 teaspoon of the filling into the center of the dumpling wrappers. Fold over the filling and crimp the edges with a fork. Place onto the baking sheet. Repeat.

4. In a skillet set over medium to high heat, add in the canola oil. Add in the dumplings. Cook for 30 seconds on each side.

5. Add ¼ cup of water into the skillet. Continue to cook for 8 to 10 minutes.

6. Remove and serve immediately.

Lemon and Chicken Dumplings

Make these dumplings whenever you are craving something on the fresh side. Perfect to make during your next family barbecue.

Makes: 8 servings

Total Prep Time: 35 minutes

Ingredients:

- ½ cup of dried sherry
- ½ cup of water
- ½ ounce of dried shiitake mushrooms, chopped
- ¾ cup of bok choy, chopped
- 1/3 cup of green onions, chopped
- ¼ cup of water chestnuts, chopped
- 1 Tbsp. of low sodium soy sauce
- 1 tsp. of salt
- 2 tsp. of ginger, peeled and minced
- 2 tsp. of grated lemon rind
- 1 tsp. of dark sesame oil
- Dash of hot sauce
- ½ pound of lean ground chicken
- 24 wonton wrappers
- 2 Tbsp. of cornstarch
- ¼ cup of vegetable oil, evenly divided
- 1 cup of water, evenly divided

Ingredients for the sauce:

- 5 Tbsp. of sweet rice wine
- ¼ cup of low sodium soy sauce
- ¼ cup of seasoned rice vinegar
- 3 Tbsp. of green onions, chopped
- 1 tsp. of chili and garlic paste

Directions:

1. In a saucepan set over medium heat, add in the sherry and ½ cup of water. Allow to come to a boil. Remove from heat. Add in the mushrooms and cover. Set aside to rest for 30 minutes or until the mushrooms are soft.

2. Drain the mushrooms and chop. Transfer into a bowl.

3. In the bowl, add in the bok choy, chopped water chestnuts, soy sauce, dash of salt, minced ginger, grated lemon rind, dark sesame oil, hot sauce and ground chicken. Stir well to mix.

4. Place the wonton wrappers onto a flat surface. Add 1 teaspoon of the chicken mix into the center of the wrappers. Fold the wrappers over and pleat the edges. Repeat.

5. In a skillet set over medium to high heat, add in 2 tablespoons of sesame oil. Add in the dumplings. Cook for 3 minutes or until golden brown on all sides.

6. Add ½ cup of water into the skillet. Cover and cook for 5 minutes. Remove the cover and continue to cook for an additional 3 minutes.

7. Prepare the sauce. In a bowl, add in all of the ingredients for the sauce. Whisk until smooth in consistency.

8. Serve the dumplings with the sauce.

Conclusion

Well, there you have it!

Hopefully by the end of this book you have found plenty of dumpling recipes that you can make completely from scratch. By the end of this book not only am I confident that you will learn the step-by-step process of making homemade dumplings but feel confident that you can make them for yourself as well.

So, what is next for you?

The next step for you to take is to begin making all of the dumpling recipes you have found in this book for yourself. Once you do that, it will be time for you to try making your own unique dumplings using everything you have learned inside of this cookbook.

Good luck!

Author's Afterthoughts

Thanks Ever So Much to Each of My Cherished Readers for Investing the Time to Read This Book!

I know you could have picked from many other books but you chose this one. So, big thanks for buying this book and reading all the way to the end.

If you enjoyed this book or received value from it, I'd like to ask you for a favor. Please take a few minutes to post an honest and heartfelt review on Amazon. Your support does make a difference and helps to benefit other people.

Thank you!

Carla Hale

About the Author

Carla Hale

I think of myself as a foodie. I like to eat, yes. I like to cook even more. I like to prepare meals for my family and friends, I feel like that's what I was born to do…

My name is Carla Hale and as may have suspected already, I am originally from Scotland. I am first and foremost a mother, a wife, but simultaneously over the years I became a proclaimed cook. I have shared my recipes with many and will continue to do so, as long as I can. I like different. I dress different, I love different, I speak different and I cook different. I like to think that I am different because I am more animated about what I do than most; I feel more and care more.

It served me right when cooking to sprinkle some tenderness, love, passion, in every dish I prepare. It does not matter if I am preparing a meal for strangers passing by my cooking booth at the flea market or if I am making my mother's favorite recipe. Each and every meal I prepare from scratch will contain a little bite of my life story and little part of my heart in it. People feel it, taste it and ask for more! Thank you for taking the time to get to know me and hopefully through my recipes you can learn a lot more about my influences and preferences. Who knows you might just find your own favorite within my repertoire! Enjoy!

Printed in Great Britain
by Amazon